D0919430

Something's Wrong!
Kids with Emotional Disturbance

Kids with Special Needs

Something's Wrong!
Kids with Emotional Disturbance

by Sheila Stewart and Camden Flath

NASHUA PUBLIC LIBRARY

JUV
616.858
STE
NPL

Copyright © 2011 by Mason Crest Publishers. All rights reserved. No part of this publication may be reproduced or transmitted in any form or by any means, electronic or mechanical, including photocopying, recording, taping, or any information storage and retrieval system, without permission from the publisher.

MASON CREST PUBLISHERS INC.
370 Reed Road
Broomall, Pennsylvania 19008
(866)MCP-BOOK (toll free)
www.masoncrest.com

First Printing
9 8 7 6 5 4 3 2 1

ISBN (set) 978-1-4222-1727-6   ISBN (pbk set) 978-1-4222-1918-8

Library of Congress Cataloging-in-Publication Data

Stewart, Sheila, 1975–
  Something's wrong! kids with emotional disturbance / by Sheila Stewart and Camden Flath.
      p. cm.
  ISBN 978-1-4222-1720-7   ISBN (pbk) 978-1-4222-1923-2
  1. Mentally ill children—Case studies. I. Flath, Camden, 1987– II. Title.
  RJ499.S796 2010
  618.92'89—dc22
                          2010004980

Produced by Harding House Publishing Service, Inc.
www.hardinghousepages.com
Design by MK Bassett-Harvey.
Cover design by Torque Advertising Design.
Printed in the USA by Bang Printing.

Photo Credits
Dreamstime: Arbon8 Pg 36; Gemphotography Pg 29; Lewis, Gary Pg 32; Lisafx Pg 37; Monkey Business Images Pg 38; Pressmaster Pg 44; Rojoimages Pg 43; iStock: nano Pg 40.

The creators of this book have made every effort to provide accurate information, but it should not be used as a substitute for the help and services of trained professionals.

Introduction

To the Teacher

Kids with Special Needs provides a unique forum for demystifying a wide variety of childhood medical and developmental disabilities. Written to captivate an elementary-level audience, the books bring to life the challenges and triumphs experienced by children with common chronic conditions such as hearing loss, intellectual disability, physical differences, and speech difficulties. The topics are addressed frankly through a blend of fiction and fact.

This series is particularly important today as the number of children with special needs is on the rise. Over the last two decades, advances in pediatric medical techniques have allowed children who have chronic illnesses and disabilities to live longer, more functional lives. At the same time, IDEA, a federal law, guarantees their rights to equal educational opportunities. As a result, these children represent an increasingly visible part of North American population in all aspects of daily life. Students are exposed to peers with special needs in their classrooms, through extracurricular activities, and in the community. Often, young people have misperceptions and unanswered questions about a child's disabilities—and more important, his or her abilities. Many times, there is no vehicle for talking about these complex issues in a comfortable manner.

This series will encourage further conversation about these issues. Most important, the series promotes a greater comfort for its readers as they live, play, and study side by side with these children who have medical and developmental differences—kids with special needs.

—Dr. Carolyn Bridgemohan
Boston Pediatric Hospital/Harvard Medical School

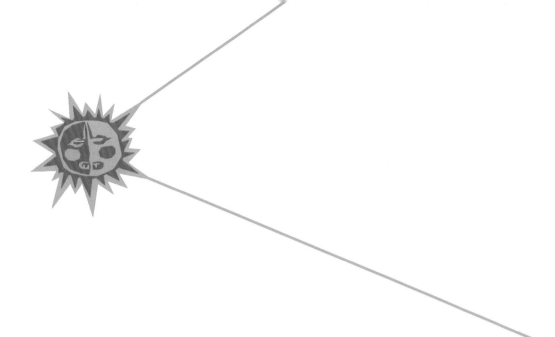

Gage glared at the big brick school building.

He didn't want to be here. No one was going to even talk to him. They were all going to hate him. It was October—not a good time to be starting a new school. Angela—his mom—had suddenly decided she wanted to move back to her parents' house.

"Come on, Gage," his grandfather said, putting his hand on Gage's shoulder. "Let's go get you set up."

Gage jerked away and then stomped after his grandfather. Before they got to the front door, the bell rang.

"Great," Gage muttered. "Now I'm late, too."

In the office, Gage stared at the floor while the secretary talked to his grandfather. She tried to talk to him a few times, too, but he glared at her.

There was a screw lying on the carpet and Gage scuffed at it with his sneaker. He sat on the floor and picked up the screw, then started scratching it against the wall that separated the secretary's desk from the outer office. At first he just made lines, then he scratched the word "Boo!" and scraped out a picture of a ghost.

"Gage! What are you doing?" His grandfather sounded shocked.

Gage shrugged, but he stood up again. He dropped the screw and scuffed it a few more times.

"Your teacher will be Mr. Frost," the secretary said to Gage. "I'll walk you down to the classroom."

"Frosty the Snowman," Gage muttered, and his grandfather glared at him.

"Straighten up and respect your teachers," his grandfather called after him as he left the office. "I

don't want to hear about you getting into the kind of trouble you did at your last school."

The secretary ignored Gage as she walked down the hall in front of him. When they walked into a classroom, a whole room full of kids stopped what they were doing and stared at Gage. The secretary introduced Gage and left, shutting the door behind her.

"We're glad to have you, Gage!" the teacher said, putting out his hand for Gage to shake.

Gage stared at the teacher's hand and didn't say anything, and the teacher put his hand down. Some of the kids started laughing.

"What are you laughing at?" Gage scowled at the class. "Don't you have some work you're supposed to be doing?"

"Ok, that's enough," the teacher said. "Why don't you take a seat over there." He pointed to a desk next to the window.

The kids kept staring at Gage as he sat down. Some of them were frowning and others looked angry. He knew it—everybody hated him already.

Two weeks later, Gage still hated school. Nobody talked to him unless they had to, and kids whispered about him behind his back. He heard some kid from his class talking about the "loser new kid." Gage wanted to cry, but instead he'd shoved the kid into the wall as he walked by.

When the school bus dropped him off at his grandparents' house that afternoon, he stomped up the front steps and went inside. He dropped his backpack on the floor just inside the door, went into the living room, and flopped onto the couch, picking up the remote control.

His grandmother came out of the kitchen. "How was school?"

"Fine." Gage flicked through the channels.

"Do you have any homework? It's always better to do it right away and get it out of the way."

Gage shrugged, his eyes still on the television. Mr. Frost had given him lots of homework—Gage figured the man hated him—but Gage didn't feel like thinking about it.

His grandmother sighed and left the room. He could hear her calling down the hall, "Angela, Gage is home!"

Angela, Gage's mother, didn't come out, but he hadn't expected her to. Angela didn't bother with him much.

The next morning, Gage's backpack lay on the floor exactly where he had left it the day before. His grandmother handed him his lunch in a brown paper bag and he stuffed it in with the papers in the backpack. He'd probably throw out the lunch anyway. She always made peanut butter and jelly, and he hated peanut butter. He should probably throw out some of the papers, too. His backpack was getting too heavy.

One day toward the end of November, Gage looked out the classroom window and saw snow falling. Soon the parking lot was covered with white. Snowflakes whirled and spun in the air, and the buildings across the street from the school looked dim and far away. Gage watched the snow in amazement. It hadn't ever snowed where he and Angela had lived before. There was something he really liked about the snow, but he wasn't sure what it was. He felt like it hid the world so that maybe he could walk into it and disappear. Then no one could ever find him again.

He'd been ignoring the world inside the classroom, the teacher's voice just a background buzz, but a tapping noise had started annoying him. The kid in front of him was tapping his pencil on his desk. Gage kicked the kid's desk.

"Hey!" the kid turned around and stared at Gage.

"Stop tapping the stupid pencil." Gage kicked the kid's desk again.

"What are you going to do about it, freak?" The kid turned tapped his pencil again, louder.

Gage grabbed the kid by the hair, pulled him backward, then reached forward and grabbed the pencil out of the kid's hand. He broke the pencil in half and broke the halves in half again. He tossed the pieces into the kid's lap and went back to looking at the snow.

The kid was screaming and the teacher was yelling. But Gage was thinking about disappearing in the snow.

Two days later, Gage sat in the school psychologist's office, waiting for Angela. The school psychologist was a pretty woman wearing black pants and a pink sweater. She reminded Gage of Angela. They'd love each other, Gage thought. His mom and the school psychologist would probably talk about the best places to get their hair done and forget he was even there.

Angela was late for the meeting, of course. She'd been mad at Gage for getting in trouble, and she had tried to persuade her parents to come to the meeting in her place. When they refused, she'd been even madder at Gage. Now, she finally breezed into the psychologist's office, her forehead wrinkled up the way it was when she was annoyed.

"I can't believe you don't have any parking spaces near the building!" Angela exclaimed. "I had to park in the bus lane."

The psychologist looked startled. "You'll need to move your car soon, I'm afraid."

"That's okay," Angela said. "I can't stay long anyway."

"I'd like to talk about the problems Gage has been having in school," the psychologist said.

Angela waved her hand. "Gage is a big boy. He doesn't need me to help him."

"But Ms. Bradley," the psychologist said, "he does need you. You're his mother."

Angela stood up. "If you're having problems with Gage at school, you're the ones who needs to deal with them. I have to go now. I have an appointment."

Gage kicked the psychologist's desk—bang! bang! bang! He waited for the lady to yell at him, but all she did was look at him. She had a funny look on her face, as though she felt sorry for him. Gage stopped banging his foot against the desk and scowled at the floor.

Nothing changed after the meeting with Angela. Then, right before Christmas, Angela left. She'd met a guy who was in a band, and she decided to go with him on a tour across the country.

Gage had bought his mom a Christmas gift, a shiny snowflake that hung from a silvery chain. He'd been imagining Angela on Christmas morning, opening the gift, saying, "Oh Gage! It's beautiful! I love you." He should have known that that would never have happened.

Gage locked himself in his room and refused to come out when his grand-mother knocked on the door. He got out the necklace's little box and stared at it—and then he opened it, ripped off the snowflake, and dropped it down the heat duct. He threw the chain across the room, then stomped on the tiny box again and again.

"Gage! Gage!" His grandmother was rattling the doorknob. "Are you okay? What's going on?"

"Go away!" He dropped onto the floor and crawled under his bed, pushing himself as far back as he could go. Then, he curled into a ball and sobbed.

The rest of the holidays were the worst he could remember. When school started again in January, Gage pretended he was sick. His grandparents didn't believe him. They made him go anyway.

As he walked down the aisle of the bus, he tripped over someone's foot. Without even thinking, he turned and punched the kid in the face.

A few days after the incident on the school bus, Gage sat in the school secretary's office, while his grandparents met with his teacher, the school psychologist, and some other people. The secretary sat at her desk, working on something without paying any attention to him. She'd given him paper and some crayons, but he didn't feel like drawing. He wondered what everyone was saying about him. He wondered if they were going to send him to juvie. Angela was always saying that's what should happen to him. Or maybe military school. Angela had said that, too.

He knew he was bad, but it seemed like people were always so mean to him that he never had a chance to be good. And nobody understood him. They didn't get how his whole world seemed gray and tired and awful—or that sometimes it suddenly turned red, and he just had to hit something. His teachers at his last school were always calling Angela to complain, but she didn't want to listen to them. He used to hope she understood how he felt—but now he figured Angela had known he was just bad. That was probably why she had left him.

Gage closed his eyes and rocked back and forth in his chair. He wrapped his arms around his body and rocked faster. His head banged against the wall. Then he hit his head against the wall again and again. The pain in his head seemed to make the pain in his heart feel better.

"Gage!" The school psychologist was between him and the wall. "It's okay, Gage. You don't need to hit yourself. We're going to help you. I promise."

The next week, a special education teacher named Ms. Gwen started coming to Gage's class to work with him. Her job, she told him, was to help him calm down and focus on what the teacher was saying. Sometimes he went to her classroom, too. Ms. Gwen was nice, so mostly he didn't yell at her, but that didn't mean he always listened either.

Then, in February, Gage got a postcard from Angela. It had a picture of a beach in California, and on the back Angela had written, "I'm having fun! XX Angela."

Gage crumpled it up and threw it across the room. After a minute, he picked it up, smoothed it out, and leaned it against his mirror. Then he sat on his bed, rocking back and forth, the way he had at school. Angela was happy she'd gotten rid of him.

The next day, the girl who sat in front of Gage left her backpack lying next to her desk. Gage tripped over it as he walked past.

"What's wrong with you?" Gage yelled.

The girl looked like she was going to cry. "What's wrong with you? You're such a bully! I didn't even do anything to you!"

Gage's face turned red, and he turned and ran out of the classroom. If he didn't leave, he would either cry or hit the girl—or both. Without thinking, he found himself heading toward Ms. Gwen's room. She had told him he could go to her room if he was ever angry or upset. He didn't know where else to go.

Ms. Gwen was sitting on her desk reading a book when Gage burst into the room.

"I hate everything!" Gage screamed. Then he flung himself onto the floor and started to cry.

Ms. Gwen let Gage cry. She didn't say anything, but that was okay, because Gage didn't want to listen to her.

"Why am I so bad?" he asked after a while, the tears still running down his face. "Everybody hates me and I'm no good at anything."

"You're not bad." Ms. Gwen looked like she actually meant what she was saying.

Gage laughed, but it was a hard, ugly sound. "I'm not stupid. I know what everybody says about me. I know I'm bad."

"Well, if people say that, they're wrong. You have so many great things about you."

Gage stared at her. "Like what?"

"For one thing, I love the way you look at the world and think about it. What you told me about the snow, for example, and wanting to disappear into it. Most people would have just seen the snow as cold and wet. *You*, though, have the soul of a poet."

Gage snorted. "You're crazy, lady. Even my own mother couldn't stand to be around me."

"Your mother has her own problems. But you didn't cause those problems." Ms. Gwen picked up her pen and began to write in her plan book. "Don't let someone tell you how to feel about yourself. I know it's hard. But when you know who you are, what other people think won't seem as important. Maybe you should get to know Gage better."

Gage squinted his eyes at Ms. Gwen, trying to tell if she was serious. "How would I do that?"

She looked up and smiled at him. "Maybe that's what you and I can figure out together."

After that, Ms. Gwen was the bright spot in Gage's life. At home, his grandparents didn't know how to talk to him. They didn't even know him, he realized. Like they didn't know he hated peanut butter. Or that he'd discovered he liked words, and he liked playing with their sounds and their meanings. Ms. Gwen had given him a book of poetry to read. He hadn't thought he would like it. But he did.

At school, he spent as much time as he could in Ms. Gwen's room. He went through stacks of magazines and cut out pictures and words, gluing them together into collages. Ms. Gwen hung his collages around her room. Looking at the designs of words and pictures somehow helped him feel as though he was getting to know who he was.

He still got into trouble a lot. Still forgot to do his homework. Still got into fights sometimes. "Are you sure I'm not just bad?" he asked Ms. Gwen.

"I know absolutely that you're not bad," Ms. Gwen answered. "And I would never, ever lie to you. I think you're pretty awesome."

Gage searched her face. "Will Angela ever come back?" His question was a test, to see if Ms. Gwen would lie to him.

Ms. Gwen sighed. "I don't know. But whether she does or doesn't, you just keep remembering you're not bad. You are interesting and talented, and you can learn to control your emotions. You can decide who you want to be."

Gage thought about it for a minute. He wanted to believe Ms. Gwen.

He felt something inside him. He flipped through a magazine Ms. Gwen had given him, searching for the right word, the right picture for what he was feeling. After a moment, he picked up his scissors and cut out a picture of the sun rising like an orange ball behind a black mountain.

Gage glued the picture on a piece of paper. He picked up a black pen and carefully wrote his own name inside the orange circle. Next, he cut out a picture of a bird and glued it so that it looked as thought the sunlight was lifting the bird into the sky. Across the bird's wings, he wrote:

I AM NOT BAD.

Kids and Emotional Disturbance

Feeling sad, angry, or *anxious* sometimes is part of life for everyone. If a kid is sad or angry more often or longer than others, though, and those feelings make behaving, learning at school, or making friends more difficult, then he may have a more serious problem. Emotions are completely normal, but when they make a child's life harder than it should be, the child may have a type of emotional *disturbance*.

The term "emotional disturbance" is used for many different *disorders* and sets of *symptoms*. A child with a mild emotional disturbance may have low *self-esteem* or signs of *depression*. If a child has a more serious emotional disturbance, they may not get

When you feel *anxious*, you feel worried or nervous.

A *disturbance* is a problem that keeps a person's mind or body from working in a healthy way.

Disorders are when a person's body or mind does not work normally.

Symptoms are the signs of a physical or emotional sickness.

Self-esteem means liking yourself, feeling good about who you are.

Depression means feelings of sadness that last for more than just a little while.

along well with others; they may break rules or act out. Children with *severe* types of emotional disturbance may have thoughts of hurting themselves or others.

An emotional disturbance lasts for a long period of time.

> *Severe* means serious or very bad.

A kid who has just had a loved one pass away, for example, may have a hard time focusing on schoolwork because she feels sad. That's completely normal, and usually, as time goes by, she will begin to cope with life again. She may still feel sad, but not so much that she can't do well in school and at home. A child is said to have an emotional disturbance, however, when her feelings last over a long period of time. She needs outside help in order to cope with her life.

If sad feelings don't go away after some time, they may be a sign of emotional disturbance.

With help from *professionals*, kids with an emotional disturbance can do better. If you know someone with an emotional disturbance, you can help, too, by being patient and kind. Although a kid with an emotional disturbance may behave differently from other kids in some ways, in most ways, he is like any other kid. He likes some things and doesn't like others. He is good at some things and not so good at others. He can be a good friend, and a fun person to play with.

> *Professionals are people who are trained to do a specific job for which they are paid.*
>
> *When an illness or emotional condition is diagnosed, that means a doctor or other expert has figured out what is wrong.*

A kid who has an emotional disturbance needs help coping with her feelings. That doesn't mean she's crazy—and it doesn't mean she's a bad person!

Symptoms of Emotional Disturbances

There are many different types of emotional disturbance, each with its own symptoms. In order to be *diagnosed* as having an emotional disturbance, a child must have one of the following symptoms for a long period of time:

- *Difficulty learning that is not caused by a learning disability, brain injury, or other medical problem.* This means that if a child has a hard time in school because she's sick, has had an injury from an accident, or has a learning disability, she would not be diagnosed with an emotional disturbance. If a child is having trouble in school and has none of these other problems, she may have some form of emotional disturbance.

> **Appropriate** *means suitable for whatever is going on at the time.*

- *Difficulty making friends, getting along with family, teachers, or other children.* A child who has serious trouble getting along with other people in the classroom, on the playground, or at home might have an emotional disturbance.
- *Feelings that seem out of place for the situation or acting out in a way that is not* appropriate. If a child reacts to something sad by laughing, for example, or becomes angry without any reason or screams at someone for some little thing, he may be showing signs of an emotional disturbance. Getting very angry sometimes is normal, but when a child acts this way toward others more often than other kids do, he might have a larger problem.
- *Feelings of sadness that last for a long period of time without any feelings of happiness.* Sadness is a part of

life—but most of us are sad sometimes and happy other times. When a kid feels sad all the time and these feelings have an effect on her school-

Emotional disturbance can make it more difficult for a kid to focus on schoolwork.

work or relationships with others, she may have an emotional disturbance.

- *Anxious feelings that cause physical symptoms.* Everyone feels nervous sometimes. When a kid feels so worried about going to school that he feels sick or exhausted, though, he may have an emotional disturbance.

Types of Emotional Disturbance

There is no single type of emotional disturbance. Instead, there are many kinds of disorders that can be described as emotional disturbance. A few examples of emotional disturbance include:

Anxiety disorder: Kids with an anxiety disorder may have feelings of nervousness or fear that keep them from focusing on everyday life. Anxiety may be caused by something scary happening in the child's life—such as being in a

Conduct is the way you act or behave.

car accident—or by troubles at home—for example, when parents get divorced. These anxious, uncomfortable feelings are normal, but if they don't fade away after a reasonable amount of time, they may be a symptom of an anxiety disorder.

Depression: If a kid is depressed or has a depressive disorder, she may feel too sad to be interested in things around her, or she may have low self-esteem. She might feel like she isn't as good as others are, or she might no longer enjoy things she used to find fun. Everyone feels sad sometimes, but if a person's mood doesn't get better with time, she may be showing signs of depression.

Conduct disorder: A child with a type of emotional disturbance called conduct disorder is likely to act out violently against others. Lots of kids get mad sometimes, but in order to be diagnosed with conduct disorder, a child must show a pattern of violent or inappropriate behavior toward others. If a child is constantly stealing from oth-

NASHUA PUBLIC LIBRARY

ers, for example, or always getting in fights or screaming at parents and teachers, he may have a conduct disorder.

Oppositional defiant disorder: Oppositional defiant disorder (sometimes called ODD) is a type of emotional disturbance similar to conduct disorder. Kids with ODD are apt to argue constantly with their parents or teachers. They may be rude to adults and refuse to obey them. One difference between ODD and conduct disorder is that kids with ODD are not likely to be violent.

> A person who is *oppositional* likes to do the opposite of whatever someone wants him to do.
>
> A person who is *defiant* does not want to do what he is told.
>
> *Psychiatric* has to do with the study of the mind and the emotions.

Schizophrenia: Schizophrenia is a severe type of emotional disturbance called a *psychiatric* disorder. Schizophrenia is a brain disease that causes people to see and hear things that are not really there. People with schizophrenia may also feel scared that someone is planning to hurt them. There is no cure for schizophrenia, but medicine can help a person live with the symptoms. Children are less likely to have schizophrenia than teenagers and adults are.

What Causes Emotional Disturbance?

Experts believe that many things together cause emotional disturbance. Certain *risk factors* make some people more likely than others to have some types of emotional disturbance. These factors include:

- Personal *characteristics*. These could be illnesses that run in a person's family, his personality, and his ability to deal with stress.

- *Caregiver* ability. Parents or other caregivers have an important part to play in a child's life. When parents aren't able to care for their child because of drug or alcohol abuse, mental health problems, or difficulties with their jobs, their

Risk factors are things that increase a person's chances of having a disease or disorder.

Characteristics are traits or details that make something or someone what or who they are.

A caregiver is someone who provides the care a child needs. A caregiver may be a mom or a dad, a grandparent, an aunt or uncle, or any adult who is responsible for the well-being of a child.

behavior may help create an emotional disturbance in their child.

- Family characteristics. The way a family communicates, how they treat each other, and whether or not they are able to help each other in times of need are all important parts of a child's life. If a kid's family has problems, those problems can often lead to an emotional disturbance in the child.

- *Peer* relationships. Kids their own age are also important to the way kids feel about themselves. Bullying, for example, can lead to emotional disturbance in young people. Emotional disturbance is never "catching," but if a child spends time with a friend who has emotional problems and treats her inappropriately because of them, she may be more likely to develop emotional disturbance as well.

- School performance. If a child has bad experiences

Kids who are bullied at school may feel worse about themselves, or even show signs of depression.

A *peer* is someone the same age as you.

at school or trouble learning new material, she may have feelings of low self-esteem or depression. Also, poor school performance over a long period of time can often be a sign of emotional disturbance.

- Neighborhood characteristics. Kids living in neighborhoods with lots of crime or where most people don't have enough money to meet their needs often have higher chances of developing some form of emotional disturbance.

Diagnosing Emotional Disturbance

Diagnosing an emotional disturbance can often be difficult. Feelings are not always easy to see. Often, kids with emotional disturbances don't know there is anything wrong. They might feel angry or sad a lot of the time without understanding that their feelings are part of a pattern.

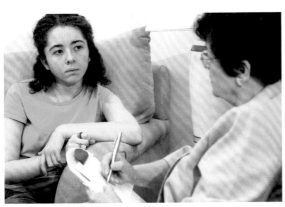

Kids who have emotional disturbance may learn to hide their feelings or begin to think that the way they feel is normal.

They might not realize that everyone doesn't feel the way they do. They might even learn to hide their true feelings from others, not wanting anyone to know how they really feel. If something at home is causing them to have feelings of depression or anxiety, children may not know to whom they should turn. For these reasons, many kids live with forms of emotional disturbances without anyone ever knowing. Sometimes it can be years before a child is diagnosed and given the special help he needs in school and at home.

> A *psychologist* studies how the mind works and helps people handle their emotions.

Many different people are trained to look for signs of an emotional disturbance. At school, teachers are often the ones who spot the symptoms of emotional disturbances.

Getting help from an adult like a teacher or school counselor can help kids with emotional disturbance succeed in the classroom.

A school *psychologist* or counselor may be the one who recognizes what is going on, or a school nurse might suspect that an emotional problem is getting in the way of a child coping with his life. Teachers and school professionals may also work with experts outside the school to help diagnose kids with emotional disturbance. A family

> A *psychiatrist* is a special doctor who treats problems with people's minds or emotions.
>
> *Classifies* means to put something in a certain category.

doctor, a psychologist, or a *psychiatrist* might help decide what is wrong in a child's life. These experts will rule out other medical problems, such as a disease, that might cause the symptoms of emotional disturbance.

Emotional Disturbance and Education

Once the school *classifies* a child as having an emotional disturbance, the school will begin making changes in the child's education. Since there are so many different kinds of emotional disturbance, there are also many different kinds of changes a kid might need. These range from working with a special teacher who understands emotional disturbance to changing the classroom setting. In many cases, teachers can change the regular classroom to best match the needs of a child. This might mean keeping harmful things out of reach of students, removing *distractions* during test taking, or changing where students sit in class. Almost all education for kids with emotional disturbances involves *positive* behavior support. Positive behavior support encourages kids to act in ways that are more appropriate.

Distractions are things that keep a person from paying attention.

Something that is *positive* is something you enjoy or like.

Special education teaches kids who have trouble learning because of some disability.

Kids with emotional disturbance may do better in a special education classroom than in another setting.

Not all kids with an emotional disturbance need *special education*, but many do. A law known as the Individuals with Disabilities Education Act, or IDEA, describes how schools decide which kids need special education. In order to qualify for IDEA, the child's condition must get in the way of him learning or taking part in school activities.

The IDEA law lists thirteen different kinds of *disabilities* that may mean a child will need special education. Emotional disturbance is one *category* that falls under IDEA.

The IDEA law requires that:

Disabilities are problems—either physical or mental— that get in the way of a person doing what other people can do.

A category is a group or a certain kind of thing.

When something is evaluated, it is examined to see in which category it belongs.

- the child has problems performing well at school activities.

- the child's parent, teacher, or other school staff person must ask that the child be examined for a disability.

- the child is *evaluated* to decide if she does indeed have a disability and to figure out what kind of special education she needs.

- a group of people, including the kid's parents, teachers, and a school psychologist, meets to decide on a plan for helping him (or her). This plan is called an Individualized Education Program (IEP). The IEP spells out exactly what the child needs in order to succeed at school.

Treating Emotional Disturbances

Children who have emotional disturbances may also get special help outside the school. Less severe forms of emotional disturbance, such as anxiety or depression, may be treatable with *therapy* alone. Other types of emotional disturbance must be treated with medicine. People with schizophrenia, for instance, may

> *Therapy* tries to solve problems by talking with a mental health expert such as a counselor or psychologist.
>
> To *prescribe* is when a doctor tells a patient to take a certain kind of medicine.

need to take medicine for the rest of their lives. The medicine can allow them learn in school, make friends, and maintain healthy relationships at home. A psychiatrist or other medical doctor will *prescribe* the right medicine to help the child.

Not all children with an emotional disturbance need medicine, but talking with a counselor or a psychologist can help most kids with emotional disturbances. Counselors and psychologists give kids a safe place to express their emotions. Often, parents will speak with a counselor as well. This can help parents learn things they can do to help their child succeed at home and at school. If problems

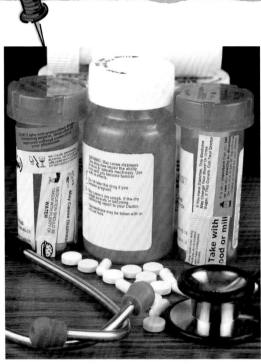

For kids with some types of emotional disturbance (such as schizophrenia), medicine is the best way to succeed.

at home are causing an emotional disturbance or adding to the stress a kid is feeling, family counseling can help kids and parents talk about their feelings and find better ways to get along.

Succeeding with an Emotional Disturbance

Kids with emotional disturbances face many challenges that others may not. Often, kids with emotional disturbance have a hard time learning in school, making friends, or getting along with their parents. All kids face *challenges*, but being a kid with emotional disturbance can be that much harder. Many kids succeed in spite of these challenges, and go on to do great things. Some emotional disturbances will get better as the child gets older and learns to cope with his life better. Other kinds of emotional disturbance may offer challenges that person must cope with for the rest of her life.

If a child has an emotional disturbance, it's not her fault! She can't help who she is or how she feels. Each person is

> **Challenges** *are things you find difficult.*

different, with different experiences and different difficulties—but at one time or another, we all cope with feelings that may seem like too much for us to handle. If someone you know has an emotional problem, make sure you are respectful to him. Making his life more difficult by teasing or bullying him will only make things worse. You can do your part by treating everyone the way you would want to be treated yourself.

Kids with emotional disturbance can benefit from positive relationships with caring adults.

Further Reading

Centre for Addiction and Mental Health. *Can I Catch It Like a Cold? Coping With a Parent's Depression.* Plattsburgh, N.Y.: Tundra Books, 2009.

Chuta, E. N. *Straight Talk to Troubled Kids: Finding Wisdom Underneath Our Pains.* Lincoln, Neb.: iUniverse, 2007.

Crist, J. L. *What to Do When You're Sad & Lonely: A Guide for Kids.* Minneapolis, Minn.: Free Spirit Publishing, 2006.

Ford, E. *What You Must Think of Me: A Firsthand Account of One Teenager's Experience with Social Anxiety Disorder.* New York: Oxford University Press, 2007.

Frank, K. *The Handbook for Helping Kids With Anxiety & Stress.* Chapin, S.C.: Youthlight, 2003.

Huebner, D. *What to Do When You Worry Too Much: A Guide to Overcoming Anxiety.* Washington, D.C.: Magination Press, 2006.

Hyman, B. M. and C. Pedrick. *Obsessive Compulsive Disorder.* Minneapolis, Minn.: Twenty-First Century Books, 2003.

Landau, E. *Schizophrenia (Life Balance).* New York: Scholastic, 2003.

Moragne, W. *Depression.* Minneapolis, Minn.: Twenty-First Century Books, 2001.

Niner, H. L. *Mr. Worry: A Story About OCD.* Morton Grove, Ill.: Albert Whitman & Company, 2004.

Wilde, J. *Hot Stuff to Help Kids Cheer Up: The Depression and Self-Esteem Workbook.* Naperville, Ill.: Sourcebooks.

Zucker, F. *Depression (Life Balance).* New York: Scholastic, 2003.

Find Out More On the Internet

American Academy of Child Adolescent Psychiatry
www.aacap.org

KidSource Online
(education and health-care information for parents and children)
www.kidsource.com

National Alliance on Mental Health (NAMI) www.nami.org

National Clearinghouse on Families and Youth www.ncfy.com

National Federation of Families for Children's Mental Health
www.ffcmh.org

National Information Center for Children and Youth with
Disabilities (NICHCY) www.nichcy.org

National Mental Health Association www.nmha.org

S.A.F.E. Alternatives (Self Abuse Finally Ends)
www.selfinjury.com

Sidran Foundation
(information about trauma-related stress disorders)
www.sidran.org

Disclaimer

The websites listed on this page were active at the time of publication. The publisher is not responsible for websites that have changed their address or discontinued operation since the date of publication. The publisher will review and update the websites upon each reprint.

Index

About the Authors

Sheila Stewart has written several dozen books for young people, both fiction and nonfiction, although she especially enjoys writing fiction. She has a master's degree in English and now works as a writer and editor. She lives with her two children in a house overflowing with books, in the Southern Tier of New York State.

Camden Flath is a writer living and working in Binghamton, New York. He has a degree in English and has written several books for young people. He is interested in current political, social, and economic issues and applies those interests to his writing.

About the Consultant

Dr. Carolyn Bridgemohan is board certified in developmental behavioral pediatrics and practices at the Developmental Medicine Center at Children's Hospital Boston. She is the director of the Autism Care Program and an assistant professor at Harvard Medical School. Her specialty areas are autism and other pervasive developmental disorders, developmental and learning problems, and developmental and behavioral pediatrics.